Animal Magnetism

KIM ROBERTS

ANIMAL MAGNETISM

WINNER OF THE
2009 PEARL POETRY PRIZE
selected by DEBRA MARQUART

Pearl
Editions

LONG BEACH, CALIFORNIA

Library of Congress Control Number: 2010929928

ISBN 978-1-888219-38-8

Book Design by Marilyn Johnson

Cover: Wooden anatomical doll from Japan, c. 1900.
Access for study and photography provided through the
courtesy of the National Museum of Health and Medicine,
AFIP, Washington, DC. Photo by Dan Vera.

This publisher is a proud member of

PEARL EDITIONS
3030 E. Second Street
Long Beach, California 90803

www.pearlmag.com

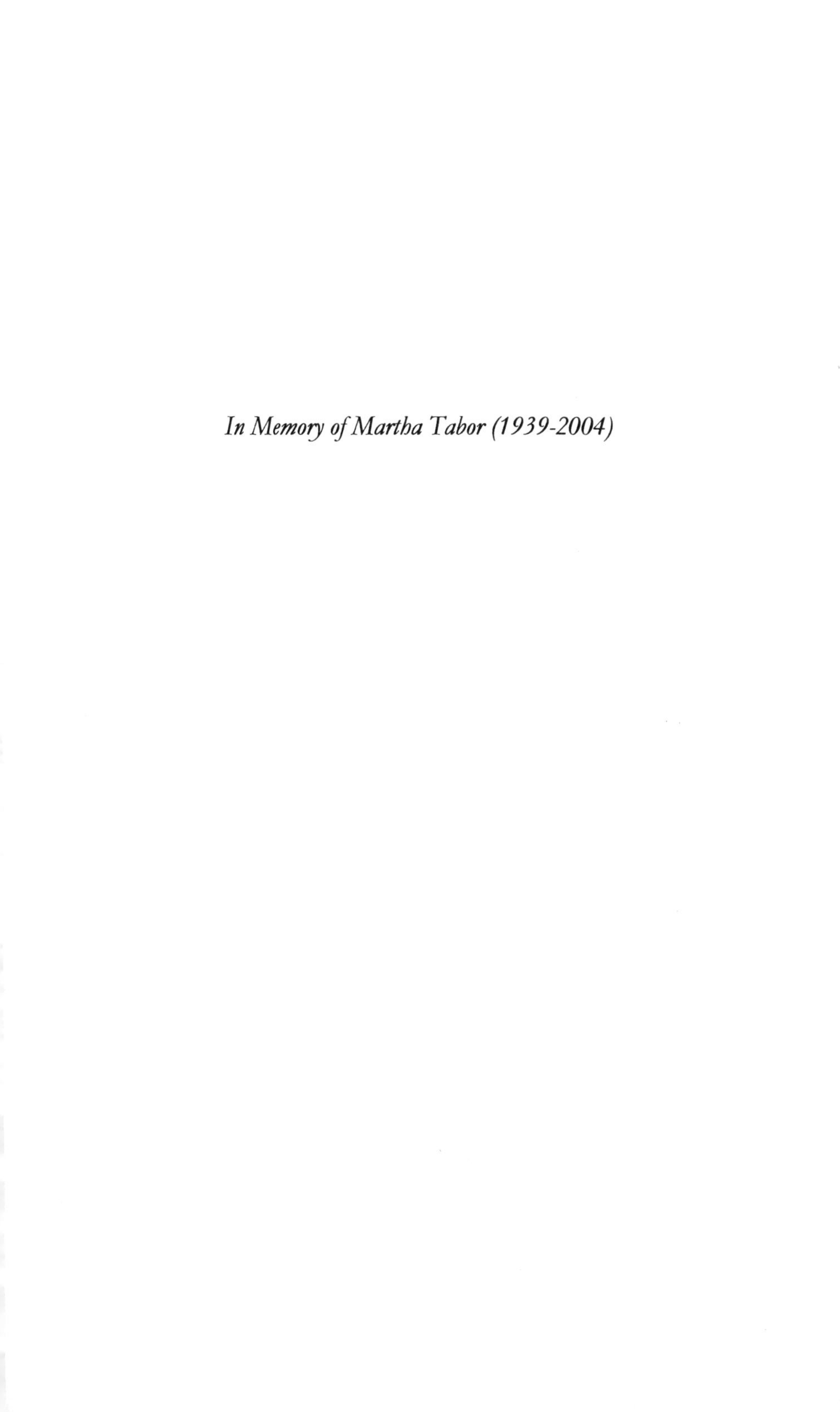

In Memory of Martha Tabor (1939-2004)

ACKNOWLEDGMENTS

The author thanks the editors of the following magazines and anthologies, where poems were first published (sometimes in earlier versions):

Attic: "Animal Magnetism"

Barrow Street: "Siamese Twins"

The Bedside Guide to No Tell Motel: Second Floor: "Seance, 1858"

Broadkill Review: "New Haven"

Caketrain: "My Imaginary Husband in Early Morning,"
   "My Imaginary Husband as the Season Changes,"
   "The Curls of My Imaginary Husband"

The Dickinson Review: "American History"

Ekphrasis: "Richard Diebenkorn's 'Figure on a Porch'"

Fieldstone Review: "IUDs"

Gargoyle: "A Private Tour"

Harpur Palate: three of the poems titled "My Imaginary Husband"

If: "Folding Chairs"

Innisfree Poetry Journal: "The Floating World,"
     "Two Studies of a Bear"

Newport Review: "'Water is Always Available to the
     Animals of the Sea'"

No Tell Motel: one of the poems titled "My Imaginary Husband,"
   "The Testicles of My Imaginary Husband,"
   "I Don't Have a Husband, I Have Nutritionist,"
   "My Imaginary Husband as a Banker,"
   "Labels"

Ocho: "Dan"

Owen Wister Review: "Boy Meets Girl"

Pearl: "Portrait of Hippocrates, or Buqrat"

Poet Lore: "Bark"

Tidal Basin Review: "On Looking at the Collections
     of Henry Wellcome"

Grateful acknowledgment is made to the The Hambidge Center, The Kimmel Harding Nelson Center for the Arts, The Mesa Refuge, The Millay Colony for the Arts, New York Mills Arts Retreat, The Ragdale Foundation, and The Virginia Center for the Creative Arts, where several of these poems were written.

For their invaluable advice and support, I thank Andrea Carter Brown, Sarah Browning, Regie Cabico, Teri Ellen Cross, Christina Daub, Barbara DeCesare, Michael Gushue, Elizabeth Poliner, Gwen Rubinstein, Gregg Shapiro, Hilary Tham, and Dan Vera.

CONTENTS

Foreword by Debra Marquart 10

I.

Blood Letting 15

Animal Magnetism 16

A Private Tour 17

The Largest Shoe 19

The Skull of Johann Gaspar Spurzheim (1776-1832) 21

The Anatomical Waxes 23

The Apothecary Doll 25

Fluoroscope 27

The American Giant and the Achondroplastic Dwarf 28

II.

Folding Chairs 33

My Imaginary Husband 34

American History 35

I Don't Have a Husband, I Have a Nutritionist 36

Labels 37

The Testicles of My Imaginary Husband 38

IUDs 39

My Imaginary Husband 40

In Memoriam: A Catalogue 41

Seance, 1858 42

My Imaginary Husband as the Season Changes 44

The Floating World 45

My Imaginary Husband 46

Boy Meets Girl 47

My Imaginary Husband in Early Morning 48

Two Studies of a Bear 49

My Imaginary Husband as a Banker 50

The Apollo Belvedere 51

The Curls of My Imaginary Husband 52

Bark 53

My Imaginary Husband 55

Siamese Twins 56

III.

Clapper 59

New Haven 60

Dan 61

Still Life with Fish, Mollusks,
    Asparagus, and a Trussed Chicken 63

The Landsdowne Herakles 65

Richard Diebenkorn's "Figure on a Porch" 66

Tobias and the Fish 67

"Water is Always Available to the Animals of the Sea" 69

Portrait of Hippocrates, or Buqrat 70

On Looking at the Collections of Henry Wellcome 72

Notes 76

FOREWORD

A few years ago while driving in my car I heard a report on NPR about a new breakthrough in medical science. By now I've forgotten what the actual discovery was, but I still recall my visceral response to a side note a scientist made about the utter darkness inside the human body—how our organs and deep tissue labor away in regions as dark as underground caverns, as absent of air as the ocean's floor.

Hearing this, I had an image of my poor liver, kidneys, heart and other necessary parts all trapped in the vessel of my dark lightless body, only brought small reserves of oxygen by my coursing blood, which was also confined to roam the endless unlit corridors of my arteries, veins, and capillaries. Right there, going home from work in the late afternoon sunshine, I was overcome with an intense wave of claustrophobia thinking about my trapped inner organs, which crested into panic when I had the thought, *Wait, I'm in there, too.* I evaded the larger ontological question about what constituted "I" in this context by bringing my sharp focus back to navigating my car through traffic at eighty miles an hour.

Since then, I've tried to explain this experience to friends, who often look upon me with amusement or bewilderment as I struggle for words. The details always fall short. However, after reading the poems in Kim Roberts' new collection, *Animal Magnetism,* I feel a little less alone and a bit more assured that someone has the wherewithal and the ability to investigate, in language that is as rich, complex, and nuanced as the human body itself, these unlit interiors of physical and emotional anatomy.

But these poems are not merely wonder cabinet exercises or explorations of morbid curiosity. They were borne, it seems, out of the author's own deep searching following a serious illness. In this way, each poem, each line, feels deeply earned. Here language takes on ritual power, in the form of incantations to organized medicine, ancient or modern ("Come, Doctor/with your iron rods,/your magnetized waters") or descriptions of the day-to-day rigors of ongoing medical procedures ("Another lab test: again my doctors/want my fluids, want to know/what stories reside in my blood").

That struggle to read the story that resides in the blood causes the narrator to travel to some of the great medical museums and anatomical exhibits of the world—The Physick House, to see the bloodletting instruments of the Father of American Surgery; the National Museum of Health and Medicine, to have a look at Eisenhower's gall stones; the International Museum of Surgical Science, to see a replica of the Fluoroscope device much like the one that x-rayed her own feet as a child to check the fit of her shoes. And here the narrator functions as a trained docent, leading the reader on a private tour of the wonders and curiosities that document the early explorations of medicine and anatomy, in which the inner workings of the body were first being opened up to the human eye.

While these poems are beautifully-made and sometimes funny or painful, they are also brimming with information. Do you know who the world's biggest shoe belonged to? Have you seen the bones of the American Giant, measured at seven feet, six inches at the time of his death at age twenty-three? Do you know where you can view a preserved section of President Garfield's spine where the bullet almost entered? The answers to these and many questions are contained within *Animal Magnetism*.

"We, who are merely human,/our shoulders soft and bare,/have such meager medicinals," one poem states, and it's because these cures and palliatives are so scarce and ineffectual that we need the steady voice of this poet—to hold us up during the panic, during the teeth-chattering, the shakes, and the willies—so that we can reach the point where, like the narrator, we can concede, "My body isn't so bad after all:/better an imperfect shell,/ ... /than nothingness."

These lines reveal the great buoyancy contained in this book, along with the stubborn clinging—to life, to love, to human connections, the most intimate of which are recorded in the "Imaginary Husband" poems. Memory and desire, past and future, seem to fuse in these poems, in the figure of the imaginary husband. We get to see him, this man of the hour, making eggs, going through the seasons, talking about the weather. We get to learn a little about the tilt of his testicles, the growth patterns of his body hair. That he doesn't last, unlike some other husbands who have the talent to "stick it out," makes him no less real. All liaisons are temporary, the poems seem to say, just as they are also indelible: "The body is a mysterious housing: it brings us pleasure, fails us daily, encloses a fragile sense of self. It is where we live. And when we die, our other half goes too."

Although the subtext of these poems asks metaphysical questions, the narrator only dares to voice it once: "Where does the soul reside?" The answer, after much searching, is only ventured: "I think it can be found in the interstices/of the brain, the dendrites/and axons, the synapses." By necessity, answers are only tentative and personal, the poems seem to conclude, contained in the negative space between what can be observed and measured, but in *Animal Magnetism*, we are invited to wander the aisles of the apothecary, searching for intangible clues.

—Debra Marquart
Ames, Iowa
July 2010

I.

BLOOD LETTING
The Physick House, Philadelphia

I turn my head away as the needle
enters that delicate fold of the inner elbow,
then look back to watch the syringe

bloom with my dark agency.
Another lab test: again my doctors
want my fluids, want to know

what stories reside in my blood.
At the Physick House, I learned
we have a total of 166 ounces

of blood in our bodies. Physick,
the "Father of American Surgery," assumed
twice that amount. A second-floor display

shows the knives he used,
the basin with the half-moon cutaway
where a patient could rest her arm.

Now his house is a museum,
all his tools and vials and paraphernalia
lined up in glass cases, and labeled.

I want to know what the labels don't reveal:
who were the patients who laid their arms
over this basin, while Physick leaned close

to cut their inner elbows, that same
fragile furrow, and let their stories flow.
I think I see a little left, a rusty stain,

a life there, hidden.

Animal Magnetism

Discovered by Franz Anton Mesmer (1734-1815)

Come, Doctor,
with your iron rods,
your magnetized water,
and bathe me. Touch me
with your fingertips,
and spark my animal essence.
Tune the fluid of my soul.

Across planetary space
electricity leaps,
the vital ether that sustains
our human organs.
In balance, the soul transmits
freely an ecstatic song.
Unbalanced, the ether
loses its harmony, harbors
sickness and decay.

I want to be healed!
Bring on your devices,
strap me in your wires. Bewitch.
Make the dry channels surge
as they once did, call down
the very powers of the black planets.
Mesmerize me.

A Private Tour

National Museum of Health and Medicine, Washington, DC

A shrunken head from New Guinea
fits in my palm.
That small. I turn him, carefully,
examine the even stitches
up the back of the neck.
The skin feels nothing like skin
but his hair is still so soft!
Inside is hollow, the skull
long cracked away and the brains
pulled out through his nostrils.
Now it is empty,
a purse of skin and hair.

From the Presidential drawer
I remove a section of Garfield's spine,
see that the bullet's path
never penetrated his spinal cord.
So what killed him was not the assassin,
but the doctor's misguided probing,
and the loss of blood.
Next to Garfield's vertebrae,
a small glass vial holds
Eisenhower's gall stones.

The wet specimen room is rarely disturbed.
Open metal shelves line
a long narrow room, cool and dark.
On a shelf labeled "Brains,"
bottles hold ornate lobes
floating in pale liquid,
like deflated basketballs.
Another shelf holds only tongues,

large and yellow, with the note
"Death from Asphyxiation
by Swallowing Foreign Objects."
An entire uncircumcised penis
and its accompanying testicles
swim in a jar, strange and innocent.

Animal parts too:
a kangaroo head, the leg
of a rooster. Like deep sea creatures,
pale, bleached out. The bottles clink
as I walk past, and murmur to themselves
at each tread, packed in, rustling,
small tremors in the liquid,
some sealed delicately in wax
over a hundred years ago.

THE LARGEST SHOE
*The Shoe Museum, Temple University School of Podiatric
Medicine, Philadelphia*

The largest shoe in the collection
came from a petite woman
       with gigantism in one leg.
The shoe, squat in its lopsided masses

of soft brown leather, crouches
in the display case,
tongue lolling.
       It is longer

than the circus tall man's
(Jack Earle's oxfords, size 18-D),
       wider than three of my shoes,
although I've always thought

my feet were enormous,
laughingly called them "boats."
Not now. Never again.
       The owner of the largest shoe

was treated at the clinic here, before finally
having her leg amputated
       (the leg alone weighed
58 pounds, I'm told).

This was only a decade ago,
but what could anyone do for her,
except fashion a shoe
       with a little more padding,

something that caused
a little less pain?
         The shoe flounders
in its plexiglass.

In the Territory of Shoes, this one
is Queen. Or was.
Now it sits alone, more metaphor
         than object.

That's what we all dream of, though:
excision. As if we could simply
         cut it away,
the enormity—

everything our bodies can produce,
the scope of our capacity
for suffering,
         the weight of mystery.

THE SKULL OF JOHANN GASPAR SPURZHEIM
(1776-1832)
The Warren Anatomical Museum, Harvard University, Boston

Spurzheim's skull
    is sliced through the brow,
  completely around,

a perfect cap, then bisected
    down the middle.
  If you put hinges on either side,

above where he once had ears,
    you could open him up
  like a treasure box.

Spurzheim made a study of brains,
    an atlas of 36 "organs"
  (Amativeness, Veneration, Marvellousness)

which controlled morality and intellect.
    His brain, one of the heaviest
  ever recorded,

would have been a source of pride
    if only he had known.
  He got so much wrong.

Tell me: is a life wrestling
    with a single misguided theory
  a wasted life?

The brain is indeed
    a treasure box:
  a little space here for perception,

an area there for volition,
                a communications center,
        a music box

with gears and flywheels,
                a pirouetting ballerina.
        The skull is a beautiful receptacle

and Spurzheim's skull,
                held upright
        on a pronged stand,

shelved behind a plate of glass,
                a slice of history,
        glows.

THE ANATOMICAL WAXES
La Specola Museum, The University of Florence

The Grand Duke of Tuscany,
Peter Leopold, opened La Specola
to the public in 1775,
the lower classes in the mornings,
"provided they were cleanly clothed,"

and the upper, "intelligent
and well educated," in the afternoon.
The public toured minerals and shells,
and the museum's star attractions,
the wax models, the wonders

of our own inner workings.
Muscles, bones, veins, tendons,
sculpted from fine Smyrna wax,
heated slowly with pigments
and turpentine, and poured

into plaster molds. Each layer
was built up by hand, modeled
under the watchful eyes
of the Grand Duke's anatomists.
The skin partially flayed, the bone

half sawn away, these models still look
so calm, eyes open, a hand outstretched,
as if they might rise
from their beds of faded green silk
and walk among us, half undone.

This one with the skull cut,
the meninges pulled away
like parchment, has one hemisphere
of the brain removed,
so you stare deep inside the skull,

contemplate the site of contemplation,
while the man stares unblinking,
contented with his sad lot.
Where does the soul reside?
I think it can be found in the interstices

of the brain, the dendrites
and axons, the synapses.
On a nearby table, another specimen brain
crawls with its red superficial arteries.
The cerebrum is divided

at the midline and the two halves
are pushed apart, revealing
the cerebellum below.
I think a soul is hovering near.
Although the Grand Duke hoped

these models would remove
the future necessity of looking at corpses,
hundreds of corpses were obtained
to make each specimen. I see souls
encased in wax, ancient souls

from the Santa Maria Nuovo Hospital,
the souls of criminals and the poor
cleanly or dirtily clothed,
in colored wax, hiding among
the thalamus and hippocampus,

among the soft and sensuous folds
of the brain, turning under,
doubling back, wax fissures
glossy and forever new
under their coat of clear varnish.

THE APOTHECARY DOLL
The National Museum of Health and Medicine, Washington, DC

Nearly four feet tall, the woman,
           carved from wood,
      painted and waxed,

has bendable joints.
           Beneath the wooden
      nipples

her flesh has been stripped
           to reveal removable organs,
      liver, kidney, colon, all—

painted mauve and ruby and ocher
           and labeled carefully
      in kanji.

What magic do you hoard, woman,
           what secret lore
      in your ankles and knuckles,

in your jape and joke,
           your vapor?
      The face is calm, eyes

open, but not too wide,
           eyelids giving
      a languorous gaze

that must have reassured
           the clients who came
      to point at where they hurt,

hoping a pill or salve
   the apothecary mixed
  in his wide-mouthed alabaster mortar

could relieve the pains
   in their own chests,
  return them to their days—

like wooden shapes so neatly classed,
   so precisely ordered—
  healed and whole.

FLUOROSCOPE
Radiation exhibit, International Museum of Surgical Science, Chicago

The X-ray showed my bones,
the tarsi lined up, the curve
of my phalanges
against the confining leather.
The shoe salesman leaned over the cabinet,
the metal viewer nestled
his cheeks and forehead
as he counted the twenty seconds,
his hand on the knob,
and I held my breath.
He was checking the fit
of my stiff new saddle shoes,
being modern, *scientific.*
Years later, when his doctor
said *cancer,* said *radiation therapy,*
the shoe salesman thought of this:
all the hundreds of children
like me, standing on the machine
while it flashed and hummed.

The American Giant
and the Achondroplastic Dwarf
Mütter Museum, The College of Physicians of Philadelphia

The American Giant has no name.
This is the first item
        in a regimen of indignities.

His skeleton was bought
in 1877 from a Dr. Foote
        for 50 bucks in Kentucky.

We know the skeleton was male,
7 feet, 6 inches tall,
        23 or so when he died.

Although only the second tallest,
a label claims he wins the prize
        for the world's longest femurs.

Inflammation or arthritis
in his final years, researchers suggest,
        flattened his bones,

kept him inactive, possibly in bed.
His enormous ribs cannot hide the extreme
        leftward curve of his deformed spine.

I imagine climbing into his display case;
I think I am exactly the right height
        to nestle my shoulders in his hip sockets.

The American Giant keeps company
with a woman standing on a doll's legs,
        an "achondroplastic dwarf,"

Mary Ashberry, 3 foot 6.
Doctors were called in 1856
        to her Richmond, Virginia, whorehouse.

She was in labor, but in that narrow
channel of her hips,
        her child's head

could not fit past.
The doctors decided to smash
        the baby's skull—

and there, the skull-chips
from the craniotomy can be glimpsed
        on the floor of the glass case.

They only managed to excise
the dead infant
        by Caesarian

hours too late.
The mother lived three more days,
        never regaining consciousness.

I come to gape.
These are our kin,
        these gimcracks on a pedestal,

these immortal souvenirs,
our forebears.
        After my own introduction

to death, the surgery,
seven weeks of daily radiation therapy,
        I feel at home

with the giant and the dwarf.
My body isn't so bad after all:
        better an imperfect shell,

even these two
might confess,
        than nothingness.

II.

Folding Chairs

Everyone had a Bob then, so we identified them by the women they associated with. Judy's Bob was sullen and grouchy and very nearly silent at every gathering; he was Judy's Nearly Silent Bob. I never understood what she thought made him worth the effort. Linda's Bob always drank too much, but he was actually a Mark; we only called him Linda's Bob. And my Bob was too volatile; I never knew what he wanted, and I'm not sure he knew either. In the end he was my temporary Bob, my Bob-passing-through, and when I left him in frustration for a Dave, those Saturday afternoon Bob-fests in Cheryl's back yard with the beer and the green folding chairs ended too. This was over twenty years ago. They all floated away, except Judy and Judy's Nearly Silent Bob, who, it turned out, was good at something after all. He knew how to stick it out.

My Imaginary Husband

My husband wields a spatula
    like a scepter,
        lords it over the eggs

toiling in the pan.
    He likes to cook breakfast
        in nothing but underwear.

As he stands at the stove,
    I sit brightly at the table
        like a well-informed citizen

(for I know better than most the doings
    of his duchy,
        the raising and lowering

of his flag). The minions
    of his hair
        creep across the elastic border

of his boxers, threatening
    to traverse the paunched
        stomach-Sahara to reach

their northern brethren.
    But they never do.
        Like so much else about my husband,

that could only happen
    in a parallel kingdom,
        a realm with no name.

AMERICAN HISTORY

Love makes us foolish.
You gave it up for ten prime years,
kept your own sad counsel.

And I? I flitted about like a dog
pent up in the house all day
then let suddenly loose in the yard

to sniff and piss, to run zigzags
from one scent to the next.
I pretended to have the memory of a dog,

living only for the present,
a new scent and I'm off again.
Ben Franklin said a single man

is the odd half of a pair of scissors.
You went like that, ten years,
hopping on one leg.

And I? I discovered one half
is still a blade, and even alone
can make a nasty cut.

I Don't Have a Husband, I Have a Nutritionist

At a gathering last night this woman, Sue, quoted her husband,
so I said, "I don't have a husband, I have a nutritionist,"
and quoted *her*. Someone asked what you'd call a group of nutritionists,
and I said, not a flock or a horde,
and Michael suggested a "buzzkill of nutritionists"

and I'm sorry Lynda, I did not defend you or your venerable profession;
instead I told them counting sodium intake
was the newest torture you'd devised for me.
Oh, how we malign those we love!
I did not say your specialty is cancer and nutrition—

that would have shut them up—
and how you've helped me through a strange and difficult time.
Instead I laughed with the others when Dan brought up Michael Pollan,
whose book *The Omnivore's Dilemma* my nutritionist
and I actually read together. Inevitably, someone mentioned the French;

someone else spoke of the foolishness of needing professionals
to tell us how to eat. Forgive me, Lynda, I turned you
into a character, as Sue always does with her husband,
a man none of us has met, allegedly a curmudgeon and a clown,
and probably someone she can't live without.

LABELS

Most people in museums spend twice as long looking at labels as looking at art.

Where did I read that?
You think: how sad for the Modiglianis.

But I like explanations
sometimes more than the things themselves.

Like: my mother sent my brother off to college
with house plants and after one semester,

when we visited his dorm room,
what was left were pots of dirt

balanced on windowsills, and labels
he'd stuck in each saying, "plant." Or that former boyfriend

from Toronto. What I liked best wasn't him
but the sign in his otherwise empty freezer:

"Scale model of Canada's frozen tundra
to make Dave feel more at home."

THE TESTICLES
OF MY IMAGINARY HUSBAND

Husband, someone packed
> your groceries poorly;
one saddlebag

hangs low. I palm it,
> feel your merchandise
move. I like to see you

bunch, uneven
> inside your jeans.
Let me rub the cloth,

hear you catch your breath.
> You own the luggage,
but I am the tourist here.

Let me hold your bags again,
> wrinkled and hairy,
dark and prophetic.

I like the way they tighten
> at my touch:
the power of resurrection

is at my fingertips.

IUDs

Dittrick Medical History Center, Cleveland

Wheels, whisks, wishbones,
silhouette of a tiny pine.

Birds in flight and fiddlehead ferns.
The uterus is a magic place.

Dark as a cave, it accommodates
any shape we insert:

circles and snakes, beetles
and bows, fossils and fleurs-de-lis.

Some are even shaped like a uterus
in miniature, amulets for warding off

miniatures of ourselves. Leaves
of a plastic ginko tree unfurl—

no end to our genius, its infinite contours.
On this scaffold we build

a barren language in plastic letters:
expandable O's, flying V's,

X's like antlers, and a range
of two-handled T's, eager to get to work.

MY IMAGINARY HUSBAND

My husband is the omphalos:
he believes when rain falls on him,
rain covers the world.
That's why, when he looks away,
his absence is total,
like the blank grey of the sky
after a heavy downpour.
All his traces disappear: shoes
piled in the front entry,
hair coiled in the shower drain,
the jangle of his ring tone.

In Memoriam: a Catalogue
Leila's Hair Museum, Independence, Missouri

After your beloved died, you clipped her hair
one last time and brought it to the artisan.
There were pattern books to look through.
One specialist threaded hair through a needle
and embroidered pictures on white silk.

Another glued hair
and pressed it into flat sheets;
these could be cut into flower petals.
The third specialty was hair weaving,
to make elaborate wreaths.

Someone is always departing.
What is more natural than grief?
It is a slack flotilla in a shifting sky,
clouds that drift and flinch.
I'll take a weeping willow on pale silk—

the tree of mourning—
I'd like a broken column—
to signify a young life cut short. *No*, you said,
*I'd like her auburn curls preserved forever
in a hair bouquet under a jar of blown glass.*

SEANCE, 1858

Based on a photograph from the exhibit "The Perfect Medium:
Photography and the Occult," Metropolitan Museum of Art, New York

The room was dark, my heart
was pumping, we sat in a circle,
men and women, there were
people I didn't know.
I was proud
of my new shoes, I was
the prettiest one, and the medium
sat me by her side.
It was dark, the room
in shadows. We sat
in a circle, our hands
touching. The medium spoke softly, I
leaned in to hear her,
she was saying the dead
were in the room with us,
their presence was strong.
I felt breathless, dizzy,
I didn't want to miss it. There was rustling,
was it the dead? The medium
tensed, the black
curtain parted, it was dark,
but I saw it, white, with hair,
and the medium placed
my hand on it. My heart tipped
on its axis, I wanted to pull away
but she held my wrist. I
was confused, dizzy,
it was dark in the room.

What was it? I thought
it might be a man, it felt fleshy,
it might be his manhood,
I screamed and let go, I upset
my chair. Another woman
screamed too, I heard furniture
moving, low voices, confusion.
I wanted to touch it again.
I reached out my hand
but the curtain had closed,
the medium was talking,
she was trying to calm us, she said
an ectoplasm was very rare.
The dead were near, we were
lucky, she said, very lucky.
Suddenly it was over, we were leaving.
What was it? I was young,
embarrassed, a little angry.
I didn't feel lucky. My shoes
were too tight. Did I seek
the spirit and touch only flesh?
Or was I so afraid of the flesh
that I chased away the spirit?
I could feel on my wrist
where she had held me
the traces of warmth
seeping away.

My Imaginary Husband as the Season Changes

Husband, I have asked
        all the wrong questions:
  now my words

skitter from me
        like fish
  before a dropped stone.

I dip my hand
        in the small of your back,
  an hourglass that measures

the early days of winter.
        Barren trees snag
  on a coil of dusty wind;

My body's rented and askew,
        as you turn to me,
  as my hand skims

your left buttock,
        but does not alight,
  does not perch, does not roost.

THE FLOATING WORLD
Ukiyo-e Wood Block Print, Smithsonian Institution, Freer Gallery of Art

I will find you here. Where
white cherry blossoms burst from ragged limbs

or on a raised wooden walkway
between terraces, where your wood sandals

clop like a horse's hoof
among bursts of early morning bird song.

I will find you here, in sheltered pavilions
against rice paper screens,

indoors and out at the same time,
outlined in black,

in a picture frame yet floating free,
a screenprint and a longing both

in delicate pinks and fading blues,
that, five hundred years later, remains as acute

as this winding stream, those craggy rocks,
our meeting place,

the tea house at the end of our graceful bridge.

My Imaginary Husband

My husband,
I clothe you in salt,

which drapes across your shoulders
in a shimmering pale wave

and falls, toga-like,
to your marvelous thighs.

I am thirsty thinking of it
but you remain immobile,

like a pharoah,
like King Tut who traveled

to the afterlife guided
by twelve painted baboons, one for each

hour of the long night.
I search your canopic jars,

breaking each heavy wax seal:
here are your two grey eyes,

still echoing with the lines
of my face; there is your tongue,

tasting of salt,
still tracing my curfew name.

Boy Meets Girl

Of all the elements on the Periodic Table,
my favorite is Molybdenum, because I love
to clack its consonants against my teeth.
It's used somehow in the production
of steel, which makes me think of Andrew Carnegie,
which makes me think of big-bellied men in suits.
When the railroad tracks met at Promontory Point, Utah,
that was a kind of love story,
if by love you mean the place where you take over
where I left off.

My Imaginary Husband in Early Morning

Husband, morning gains, and daybreak takes the sky. Slowly, in the bed,
you turn
to wake, the mattress a craft dislodged in dream

that drifts back to the new light's dock. We break from dark's flotsam,
tongueless,
listing on our sides, as sleep laps against

the calling day. We sleep to meet ourselves on an unknown shore.
We wake to our names.

Two Studies of a Bear

The larger, darker, hairier one
                has such a huge hump,
        his bearness

seems to be carried
                entirely in his haunch.
        The other, paler (younger? female?)

is too flat-backed, too elongated.
                The realer bear
        is too little bear:

she's bland and pale and flat.
                While he leers darkly,
        paws the yellowing vellum

with his vicious crescent claws,
                she remains empty-eyed.
        She remains a sketch.

Pisanello drew this in the 1430s,
                and it is still the truth:
        the grand gesture, the exaggeration,

the coiled ferocity,
                the suspicion,
        its hirsute and towering shoulders,

will always crush, will always conquer
                a waggish fidelity
        to fact.

My Imaginary Husband as a Banker

Husband, I vouchsafe to you
              my hundred odd obsessions;
          in return I let you barter

your old stories three,
              four times.
          I send you out for garbage bags

and you return with dish soap.
              Home from a trip,
          your briefcase explodes

its dividends of yellowed quotes
              across our bedroom floor.
          Each night, your stocks accrue

a deep and dreamless sleep
              spooning next to my bonds.
          In our economy

of quirks and secrets,
              habits and rituals,
          it seems an even exchange.

THE APOLLO BELVEDERE

By the main entrance to Caesar's Palace
on the Vegas strip, he keeps a sharp eye
on the cabs and limos, the porters
in crisp white suits with gold epaulets.

The Apollo Belvedere towers above me.
Yet he appears weightless, his left foot
touching down lightly on the tip
of his sandal, as if he might leap

off his pedestal and fly.
Those lordly curls, that sidelong gaze,
the fig leaf teasing the imagination.
In this version, he is made whole again,

two muscular arms, two graceful hands.
He has found his long-lost bow.
That's what they do here, among
the endless clanging of the slots:

they fix us.

THE CURLS
OF MY IMAGINARY HUSBAND

Resemble eddies that meander
over his scalp and cascade
toward his shoulders.

I like how they refute Newton's
law of gravity, and fill my palm
with soft half-moons.

I like their lack of purpose:
their frivolity, the way, between haircuts,
he flips them from his eyes

and how, like the climbing ivy,
they shake in the wind,
and quiver from a pivot.

BARK

The sound fills the front yard,
                    expanding,
bouncing against the wooden fence
          and rising on a sluice of wind:

a satisfied bark,
                    smug
with the fulfillment of its destiny,
          full throated, repetitive, and sharp.

Clearly the yard
                    can't contain it;
an agent of Heavenly Providence,
          it takes off down the block.

It wakes the sleepers, drowns televisions,
                    bangs
at strangers' doors.
          Very soon the vagabond bark

encompasses a grid of streets, a school,
                    a park
with the astonished mouth
          of a stringless basketball hoop.

The rudderless bark
                    knows no weather,
can't distinguish night from day.
          It is a thing unstoppable

until it stops, and then
               the neighborhood
turns its windows inside out,
          the very cars are hushed

knowing a great presence
               has abandoned
its mechanics, and we turn to one another
          in hoarse silence.

MY IMAGINARY HUSBAND

My husband always talks
            about the wind
      that shakes up the trees;

he's got sixteen
                  different ways to describe
      how the leaves chatter.

I can think of
                  a half dozen sounds
      I'd rather hear.

He dances in splayed sneakers
                  across asphalt's brittle trust
      while the trees declaim,

wagging their fingers,
                  and the alley's loose chain link
      rattles like a guard dog.

When everything looms—
                  a storm, a fight—
      my husband is bouyant;

he loves most the frayed
                  and dangerous edges
      that threaten to call us out of our names.

Siamese Twins

Chang and Eng shared a liver.

For eight years, they toured America and England performing acrobatics (although denied entry to France: officials feared their malady would spread to pregnant women).

In America, they always appeared with the image of an eagle and the motto, *Union and Liberty, one and inseparable, now and forever.* Like two states in a united nation. Like their home state, North Carolina,

where they retired at 28, became farmers, married sisters, and between them sired 21 children.

Emerson once wrote that life *cannot be divided or doubled. Any invasion of its unity would be chaos. The soul is not twin-born, but the only begotten . . .*

I wonder how they taught themselves that delicate dance: when to fuse, when to be separate, how to make their own privacy.

The newspapers wrote that Eng died of fright, waking next to his dead brother in the dark. But really Chang died from a cerebral clot, and when blood pooled in his body, Eng bled to death.

The body is a mysterious housing: it brings us pleasure, fails us daily, encloses a fragile sense of self. It is where we live. And when we die, our other half goes too.

CLAPPER

Like the clapper of a church bell,
under a cover of skin,
rising slightly from a dark chamber
—tonsil—one day you were revealed.

Alive, under a single sheet,
you were unveiled.
Scalpel flashing beneath the white bulb,
five hours pulling out the cancer.

By the white light a promise
from the depths of my body,
from neck to heart,
nerve endings branching under the flensing.

With what precision the surgeon
removed and extinguished
the last resounding of a small bell,
a morning star.

New Haven

You might see an elephant
plowing a wheat field, some mild evening
in early fall,
> just past New Haven,

timed for the evening commute.
If you press your face against
the window-glass, you can see
> in the distance

P.T. Barnum's mansion, Iranistan,
iced like a confection—
with turrets and gilded domes
> and four stories

of wrap-around porches
dripping with carved scrollwork.
The Old Humbug's not at home.
> He's off to Europe

with his pretty young niece
to buy us something new—
dog-faced boys, bearded ladies,
> midgets, Siamese twins.

DAN

1.

Dan snaps on the car radio and a woman with a high nasal voice is saying something about unity, the oneness of the universe, how everything we can perceive becomes internalized, and Dan says:

*We are mountains. We
are trees. We are post office
boxes. We are gum.*

I turn it into a haiku, counting the syllables on my fingers. *Why so punchy this morning?* I ask. *We are coffee,* he answers.

2.

I go upstairs to change and Dan, all alone in the living room, in an operatic tenor, sings the music from *Oklahoma,* his voice quavering at the high notes, and booming at the lows, joy rumbling through the floorboards and up the stairs. His *corn is as high as an elephant's eye,* he informs the couch and the coffee table, the tiers of dazzled books no longer slumped in their assigned seats.

3.

When Dan can't remember the name of any small thing—a power strip, say—he will call it by a fake Ikea name, like *Geflurden-morven,* or *Megroden-min-hasser.*

4.

Dan drives past the statue of Samuel Gompers, President of the American Federation of Labor, on Massachusetts Avenue. Gompers sits on a throne-like plinth, surrounded by half-dressed allegorical figures. *I just like saying "Gompers,"* I tell him. He thinks a moment, then decides it would make a good name for a candy. *Labor-endorsed licorice-flavored gompers!* he says.

5.

Driving at night with Dan and Pete, I say that I've never met a
Barry who wasn't bitter. Pete asks, *What about Barry Manilow?* Dan
sings a line, *Oh you came, and you gave without taking* . . . Then he says
Manilow is infectious; he's like bubonic plague. I ask, *If Rod Stewart
were a disease, what would* he *be?* Dan answers, *Scabies.*

STILL LIFE WITH FISH, MOLLUSKS, ASPARAGUS, AND A TRUSSED CHICKEN

1st century, Museo Archeologico Nazionale di Napoli

Darling fragment,
> how you suggest perfection,
little fresco, rescued

from the ash of Mt. Vesuvius
> that hardened around you
like concrete.

The asparagus spears huddle
> to talk strategy, wrapped
in a piece of brown twine.

Dabs of white on their faces
> make each stem appear
newly washed.

The squat brown package
> must be the chicken.
Most amazing

are the heaped plates of fish,
> ruffled fins
glistening pink

and the squid that stands
> on tentacles
and winks his black eye.

When the ash was tunneled through
> centuries later,
a world of beauty

and abundance was revealed,
                where villa owners kept
        private fishponds, adorning

the waists of their favorites
                with gold rings
        so that Cicero complained

some senators lavished more attention
                on their mullets
        than on affairs of state.

Or this fragment, *Still Life*
                with Writing Implements
        —so charming—

a wax writing tablet
                with four leaves,
        triangular scraper

for erasing mistakes,
                double inkwell in soft gold
        with one side open,

reed pen leaning,
                and a scroll of papyrus
        unspooling, scored

with the faded letters
                of a beautiful story,
        half told.

THE LANDSDOWNE HERAKLES
The Getty Villa, Malibu, California

I thought of you, recovering from your surgery,
here where the scent of rosemary hangs
in the air, the smell
of invulnerability.

For the hide of the Nemean Lion
can't be pierced by weapons.
He clutches a knobby club in his left
and the lion skin in his right.

The lion still has its teeth,
its claws, the curl of its wondrous mane,
and Herakles stares at the wall,
contemplating his next victory

among the distant hills,
his penis missing, his torso perfect.
Herakles wrestled the lion, strangled it,
skinned it with its own claws—

the first of his twelve
fabled labors—then wore it
like a magic shield
atop his heroic shoulders.

Getty built his Herakles
a temple with a coffered dome
like the Pantheon's,
and a view of the Pacific.

How I wish I could give you that pelt.
We, who are merely human,
our shoulders soft and bare,
have such meager medicinals.

Richard Diebenkorn's "Figure on a Porch"
Oakland Museum of California

We make a landscape
from flat bands of color:
blue at the top is always sky,
the orange of the porch
is the ground on which we stand,

looking out across the fields.
It is human to reason,
to try to make sense
from the abstract. It is human
to place ourselves on the porch.

The hot colors of the lowest band
rush toward us, as hot colors
tend to do: masculine
orange and red reach out,
invite, while the cool greens and blues

recede: private, female.
The figure on the porch is a woman.
Her head might be a smudge,
a thumb print—she balances
between figure and mere shape—

but she stares out over the water
as we do, looking at her looking
at bands of color, stripes on a canvas,
light caught but not static,
trapped but still shimmering.

TOBIAS AND THE FISH
"All is fish that cometh to net." —*Proverbs*

What is this fish attacking the foot of Tobias? *Grab it*, says Raphael,
who is actually an angel disguised as a man,
so Tobias reaches into the river and hauls it up with one hand.
The fish is large, scales glinting in the sun, the row of tiny white teeth
sharp as any sawblade. Its gills tremble in the air.

Raphael grabs a knife and guts the fish, holding it against the muddy bank
of the Tigris. *There is strong medicine in a fish,*
Raphael says, cutting out the liver, gallbladder, and heart.
We will take these on our journey.
That night, they seek out the house of Raguel,

a distant relative of Tobias. He lives along the road to Media
with his wife and cursed daughter. Sarah, young, suffering, beautiful,
greets them at the door. *I have heard about you,*
Tobias says. *Is it true that you have buried seven husbands?*
Sarah's cheeks flame. Raphael, always quick with advice, says,

Marry her; end her torment! Tobias turns in horror.
But a devil pursues her! All her husbands
die on their wedding night, before they reach her bed.
Raphael nods. *Do you still have the organs of that fish?*
Raguel welcomes the travelers. His wife prepares food and drink.

And while Raguel draws up a wedding contract in his finest Ptolemaic script,
and Sarah's untouched breasts tremble like gills
as she unrolls her mattress, Raphael shows Tobias
how to burn the liver and heart with incense
in his marital chamber. *This will drive the devil from her*, he says,

slicing the fish's shiny organs.
And the gallbladder? asks Tobias, for he is fearful.
What if Raphael is wrong? *Don't be silly*, says Raphael, *the gallbladder
is for something else entirely. We will use that later,
to cure your father's blindness.*

"Water Is Always Available to the Animals of the Sea"

*From an educational sign at the Marine Science Center,
Port Townsend, Washington*

Moon face, dog face,
bloody fist face, face like a pumpkin pie.
Angle of fin. Flick of tentacle.
Then the frilled distress of gill,
the copper scent of despair:
Why speak of it? Why speak of its absence either?

Air is cruel, and some things are fat
with self-prophecy; "obvious"
is too easy and flat a word to serve.
Banana face, buck tooth, saw nose,
fan dancer, flirt.
There is only the present; water may ebb

or flow but why measure a constant?
Who takes comfort in what's not noted?
Tomorrow, tomorrow, yells a man on the shore.
We think time is our element. We dip our nets
into the sea, a silver line, a lure—
moon face, dog face, hope like an open door.

PORTRAIT OF HIPPOCRATES, OR BUQRAT

from The Falnama *of 1703, Topkapi Palace, Istanbul*

O augury seeker,
> *know and be aware.*
In the book of divination,

Hippocrates rides the *simurgh,*
> a mythical bird,
as he returns to his home

carved from emeralds
> on Mount Qaf.
With his white turban,

scholar's dark beard,
> and bright orange robe,
he looks over one shoulder

and strokes the bird's
> golden tail feathers
as she flits through an azure sky

between eddies of clouds.
> Healer of the sick,
Builder of the first hospital,

Master of alchemy,
> astrology and magic,
I have prepared myself

for your prognostication
              with bathing and prayers,
        opened the book in my blindness,

opened my heart in hope
              and placed my body,
        my wounded body, in your hands.

ON LOOKING AT THE COLLECTIONS OF HENRY WELLCOME

The British Museum, London

1.

Votive offerings used in prayers for healing
in the shape of feet, hands, eyes,
viscera, genitalia, uteruses,
bladders, kidneys, tongues—
all in ceramic, and highly detailed,
made in ancient Greece and Rome.
Hippopotamus ivory dentures
on dainty porcelain stands, a box of glass eyes,
a guillotine blade used during the French Revolution,
Egyptian canopic jars,
17th century clappers used by lepers
to warn people of their approach,
artificial limbs, arrays of obstetrical forceps
and amputation saws.

2.

After his death, they found crates
that had never been opened.
The treasures lay inside, packed
in straw: human remains
from the Sudan, the dearticulated bones
side by side in the dark; German manuscripts
on alchemy; figurines from New Guinea shut in boxes
as if in mass graves. He bought obsessively,
the buying was most important.
That, and the idea of his museum
for the study of the roots
and foundations of medicine.
I am not merely "gathering curios,"
he told his exasperated wife.

3.

Ever since our marriage, she wrote, *the greater part*
of our time has been spent in places I detested
collecting curios, sacrificing myself—
And for what? Filigreed amulets
of open hands from Tunisia?
Canopic jars for a dead man's intestines?
Or those unspeakable miniature women?
Their heads resting on ivory pillows—
their hair arrayed in perfect curls,
little smiles playing at the edges of their lips—
how can they look so serene
when anyone can reach right in
and remove their intestines, reach right in
and evict their tiny ivory hearts?

4.

A pair of slippers owned by Florence Nightingale.
Charles Darwin's walking stick,
topped with a tiny skull carved in ivory,
two emeralds for the eyes.
A snuff container made from an entire ram's head
hollowed out, so the snuff replaces the brain,
resting on three silver wheels.
A radiograph (Germany, 1908) of a child born bearing
two spines and two heads. Ceramic women,
no bigger than my palm, with removable fetuses.
A tobacco resuscitator from 1774:
one of a series of kits placed along the banks of the Thames
at regular intervals, to revive drowning victims
by injecting smoke into their rectums.

5.

In my home, too, there is a collection
of medical oddities, votive offerings
used in prayers for healing:
latex gloves, alcohol prep pads,
pleated white paper face masks,
boxes of heparin lock flush solution in 5-inch syringes,
a clear bag of single-use sodium chloride injection packs,
9 volt batteries,
filters with add-on siphon valves
placed along the banks of the dining table,
interlocking 20g precision glide needles,
4 central-line kits rich in passionate symbolism,
one wide-mouthed red plastic container
marked "biohazard."

6.

Nine years passed before Syrie Wellcome
left Henry behind. She persevered
as long as she could. I know
the cost, how it made him
a little less human. But his passion
was larger than himself;
it swallowed him up. Tincture of bryony,
infusion of capsicum. An ivory model
of a human ear. How could he stop?
And now I live with someone else's obsession,
the collection on my dining room table,
bandage tape, 3 kinds of antiseptic lotion,
needles in several sizes,
a little museum, the self-absorption of the dying.

7.
What happens to avid collectors?
After a while, they cease defining themselves
by the objects they possess, and the objects
seem to possess them instead, as if the human
becomes a vehicle for inanimate fulfillment.
As the definitions of their obsessions
get more and more refined, more exacting
(an optometer with 38 lenses), the humans,
under the weight of their project, like butter
at room temperature, go soft around the edges.
They are fascinating.
They themselves become a display.
An extreme version of something inherently human.
All that derelict beauty.

8.
A mania for objects, for creating a world—
a metaphor for the world—a smaller cosmos,
but controlled, and controllable.
Is it triggered by loss? Fear of abandonment?
Depression? As if the wonders of the little world
had magic properties, as if these fragments
on display could keep the body whole,
could stop time, stop death: keep the blood
moving through the veins, the food digesting,
keep the muscles and the bones from splitting
and the delicate webbing of skin—
a fragile cabinet whose textures imply
so much activity beneath the surface—
were somehow under our own control.

NOTES

Section I:

I first began visiting medical museums when I was caring for my friend Martha Tabor, who was dying of cancer. My interest continued after my own cancer diagnosis and treatment. My deep gratitude to my doctors: Dr. Catherine Picken, Dr. Greg Sibley, Dr. Nirupma Rohatgi, and especially to my big brother, Dr. Ken Roberts. Unlike Martha, who succumbed to her cancer in 2004, I am now considered cured.

"Blood Letting": Philip Syng Physick (1768-1837), known as the "Father of American Surgery," was a proponent of bloodletting. His name is a corruption of the older English name Fishwick.

"A Private Tour" and "The Apothecary Doll": Thanks to the former Senior Curator of the National Museum of Health and Medicine, Dr. Jeff Reznick, for his hospitality.

"The American Giant and the Achodroplastic Dwarf": Achondroplasia usually results in extremely small limb formation on a normal-sized body. The disease interrupts the normal formation of cartilage.

Section II:

"American History": Quote from *The Autobiography of Benjamin Franklin* (1868).

"In Memoriam, A Catalogue": Prior to the advent of photography, the custom of creating mementoes from a departed loved one's hair was a common practice.

"Boy Meets Girl": The place where the Union Pacific and Central Pacific rail lines met to form the Transcontinental Railroad was marked with the driving of a golden spike on May 10, 1869. There is, alas, no longer a continuous railroad track running through there.

"Siamese Twins": Quotes from Daniel Webster (from his famous Congressional speech in 1830) and from *The Conduct of Life* by Ralph Waldo Emerson (1860).

SECTION III:

"Portrait of Hippocrates, or Buqrat": *The Falnama* is a Book of Omens, an Islamic illuminated manuscript from the 16th century that was used for divination. Only four are known to still exist; I saw them on display at the Smithsonian Freer Museum.

"On Looking at the Collections of Henry Wellcome": Wellcome was an American who made his fortune by introducing medicines in tablet form (in accurately measured and easily administered doses) in England. He began his obsessive collecting in approximately 1895, with the intention of creating a museum of the history of medicine.

KIM ROBERTS is the author of two previous books of poems, *The Kimnama* (Vrzhu, 2007) and *The Wishbone Galaxy* (WWPH, 1994). In 2000, she founded the acclaimed online journal *Beltway Poetry Quarterly*. She is editor of the anthology *Full Moon on K Street: Poems About Washington, DC* (Plan B, 2010), and author of a nonfiction chapbook *Lip Smack: A History of Spoken Word Poetry in DC* (Beltway Editions, 2010). Ms. Roberts is the recipient of grants from the National Endowment for the Humanities, the DC Commission on the Arts, and the Humanities Council of Washington, DC. Individual poems of hers have been translated into Spanish, Portuguese, German, and Mandarin. She has been awarded writers' residencies from twelve artist colonies. Her website: www.kimroberts.org.